出塵

Transcending the World

Transcending the World 出塵 : Pearls of Wisdom by the Venerable
Master Hua
Illustrations by: BTTS

Published and translated by:
       Buddhist Text Translation Society
       1777 Murchison Drive,
       Burlingame, CA 94010-4504
       www.drba.org

☐ 2004   Buddhist Text Translation Society
       Dharma Realm Buddhist University
       Dharma Realm Buddhist Association

10 09 08 07   10 9 8 7 6 5 4 3 2 1

Printed in Taiwan

Library of Congress Cataloging-in-Publication Data

Hsuan Hua, 1908-
 Transcending the world : pearls of wisdom of the Venerable Hua
 / Buddhist Text Translation Society.
    p. cm.
 ISBN 978-088139-865-6 (alk. paper)
1. Wisdom--Religious aspects--Buddhism. 2. Conduct of life.
3. Virtue. I. Buddhist Text Translation
Society. II. Title.

 BQ4380.H75 2004
 294.3'444--dc22
                          2004051956

献給您 —— 志如松柏耐寒暑
願似蓮華離塵垢

Dedicated to you —

Our resolve is as the evergreen enduring the seasons.
Our vows are as the lotus lifting itself above the mud.

為什麼世界不和平？
就因為人人貪心太大了。
大人物就有大的貪心，
小人物就有小的貪心，
每一個人有每一個人的貪心，
一個國家有多少人，
就有多少貪心。
所以若要人人變成一個平安的人，
先要從心裡做起，
心裏沒有貪心、
沒有鬥爭、
沒有瞋恨、
沒有痴心，
世界就會和平了。

Peace

Why isn't the world peaceful?

It is because everyone is too greedy.

Great people have great greed.

Small people have small greed.

Each person has his own greed.

However many people

there are in a country,

that is how many greedy people there are.

So if people want peace,

they must start from their own hearts.

If people's hearts are not greedy,

are not contentious,

are not full of hatred,

and are not delusion,

then the world will be peaceful.

Small people have small greed.

世界為什麼有戰爭？
就是因為我們心裏天天都在那兒戰爭，
天天都在那兒和自己過不去，
這真是一個很矛盾的行為。
心裏的嫉妒障礙、
恨怨惱怒煩都消除了，
這就是心裏的原子彈、
核子彈都消滅了。

因此，每一個人都要知道——
世界的大戰爭，
就由我們心裏的小戰爭引起的。
所以我們必須先把自己的小戰爭平息了，
大的戰爭才會沒有。

9

Ceasing

Why are there wars in the world?
It is because every day
we are at war in our hearts.
We cannot get along with ourselves.
This really is contradictory behavior.
If the jealousy, obstruction, hatred,
and anger in our hearts cease,
it is like an atom bomb
or nuclear bomb disappearing.

Therefore, everyone should know
that all the big wars
in the world start from the small wars
within our hearts.
So we must first subdue the small wars
within our hearts,
and then the big wars will cease to be.

有人說世界壞了——
這是一個錯誤的說法，
世界根本就沒有壞。

有的人又說，
世界既然沒有壞，那是人壞了——
這也是一個錯誤的說法，人也沒有壞
那是什麼壞了呢？

是人心壞了。
人心壞了，所以把世界弄壞了，
把人也都弄壞了。
心壞了就會造惡業，
造惡業就會受惡報，
受惡報就造成世界不平安。
所以要想人好、世界好，
先要從人心做起，
人心若好，世界就沒有戰爭了。

Goodness

Some people say that the world is going bad.
That is incorrect. The world cannot go bad.
Some people say
that if the world is not going bad,
then must be people going bad.
That is also incorrect.
People cannot go bad.
Then what is going bad?
It is people's hearts.
Because people's hearts are bad,
they make the world bad and make people bad.
When a person's heart is bad, he creates bad karma.
Bad karma then evokes unpleasant retributions.
Unpleasant retributions create discord in the world.
So if you want people to be good
and the world to be good,
you must start with the hearts of individuals.
When people's hearts are good,
there will be no more wars in the world.

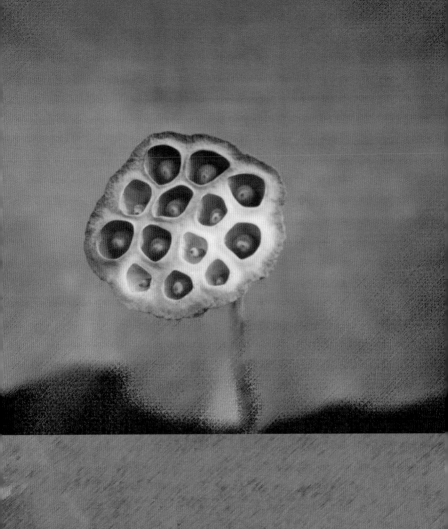

脾氣的根本，不是從吃東西來的，
也不是從天來的、地來的，
更不是從什麼氣候來的，
而是從自己這個無明來的。

無明從什麼地方來的？
就是自私在後邊作怪。
所有的煩惱，
都因為自私在後邊支持著，
所以就有很多脾氣、很多煩惱。
因為怕自己吃了虧，
怕對我有所損害，
所以才要發脾氣、要爭。
如果你「不爭、不貪、不求、
不自私、不自利」，
什麼脾氣都會沒有了。

The Source

Our temper does not come from
our food or heaven
or earth or the climate,
but rather from our own ignorance.
Where does ignorance come from?
It is our selfishness working behind the scene.
All afflictions are supported by selfishness.
That's what causes us to have a bad temper
and many afflictions.

We are afraid of taking a loss or of being hurt,
so our tempers flare and we start to fight.
If we can avoid fighting, greed, seeking, selfishness,
and pursuit of personal advantage,
we will not have a temper.

Everyone has one hundred hearts.

每個人都有一百個心——
在這一百個心裏頭，
只有一個壞心，九十九個都是好心。

可是呢——
所有的好心都在底下，
而那一個壞心卻跑到上面來了。

所以——又自私，又自利，不肯吃虧，
不肯利人，不肯代眾生受苦。

我們若把這一個壞心給翻下，
不要跑到上面來，
這就是菩薩的心腸。

Hearts

Everyone has one hundred hearts.
Among these one hundred hearts
only one is bad;
the other ninety-nine are good.

However, all the good hearts are buried
at the bottom,
and the bad heart races to the top.
Thus we become selfish and self-benefiting,
are unable to take a loss or help others,
and are unwilling to take
on suffering for others.
If we overturn this bad heart
and don't let it rise to the top,
then we will have the heart of a Bodhisattva.

捨

布施就要拿出真心來，
你不能捨得的才要捨。
所謂捨錢如割肉，
一般人很難發出布施心，
若能拿出真正的力量來做布施，
捨不得的能捨，那就是真心的布施。
你若捨得的，那就不是真心，
這也不能說沒有功德，
但不是那麼純粹，力量也沒有那麼大。

Giving means sincerely parting
with what you cannot part with.
There is a saying, donating money
is like cutting off your flesh.
Most people cannot give rise
to a generous heart.
If one can sincerely practice charity
and donate what is hard to give up,
that is true giving.

If one gives with reservation,
that is not true giving.
Although such giving
is not without merit,
the merit is not so great.

Giving

「有德真富貴，無道是清貧」，
一般人以為金銀珠寶才是富貴，
其實不是，這是外在的財寶，
隨時都會被人搶去。

古德說：「富潤屋，德潤身。」
人無道，就是真正的貧窮。
這個「貧」字，
是由「貪」字演變出來的，
因為貪得無厭而結果貧窮。

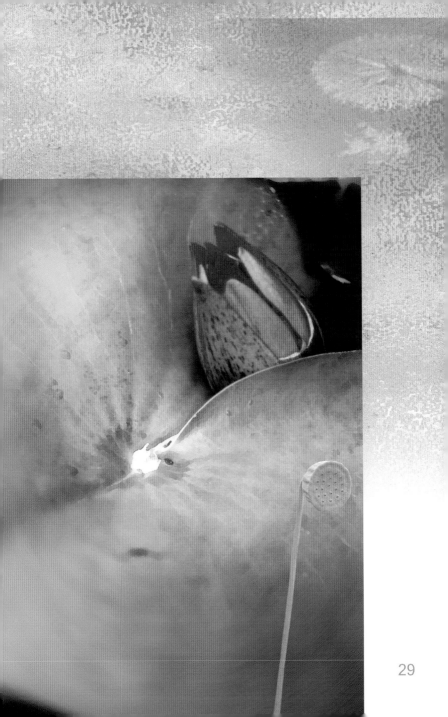

Poverty

One with virtue is truly rich.
One without the Way is truly poor.

Most people believe that silver,
gold and precious gems represent wealth.
Actually they do not.
These are just external trappings of wealth,
which can be taken away at any time.

The ancients said,
"Wealth benefits one's home;
virtue benefits one's body."

Those without the Way are truly poor.
The Chinese character for poor 貧 (*pin*),
is derived from the Chinese character
for greedy 貪 (*tan*).
That's because when you are too greedy,
you become poor.

在這世界上，有樂就有苦：
樂是苦的因，苦也是樂的因。
所以我常說：
「受苦是了苦，享福是消福。」
例如，
「十年寒窗苦，一舉成名天下知」，
這是所謂「苦盡甘來」，
但這個樂是從苦惱換來的。

又好像種田的農人，
現在用機器來種田，
沒有出那麼多的力量，但是需要汽油；
若是能源缺乏了，
恐怕機器又行不通了，
又要用回人力，
這都是苦惱無量，不知道有多少苦惱。

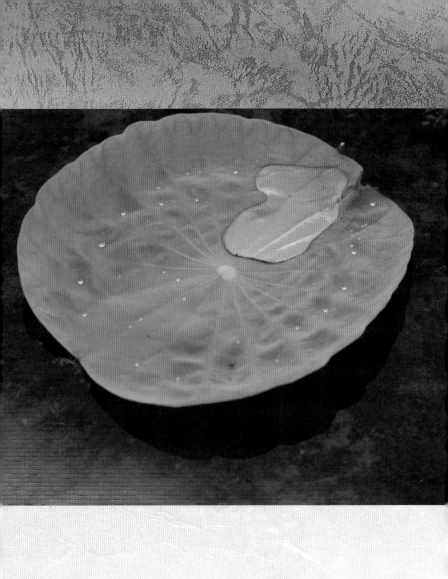

Suffering

In this world, wherever there is joy,
there is also suffering.
Joy is the cause of suffering.
Suffering is also the cause of joy.
So it is often said,
"Enduring suffering puts an end to suffering;
enjoying blessings uses up blessings."

There is an ancient Chinese saying,
"Suffering as a poor student studied hard for ten years,
as soon as he is successful,
he is famous throughout the world."
Another saying is,
"When suffering ceases, joy arrives."
But this joy comes from suffering.

It is like the farmer who tills the land.
He can use machinery now to plow his field,
and he doesn't have to expend so much effort.
But he needs gasoline.
If all the natural resources are used up,
he won't be able to use his machinery
and will have to return to manual labor.
Then he will have unlimited suffering,
untold suffering.

眾生貪著五欲，
總覺得五欲是不錯的：
就好像小孩子吃糖，
吃完了一塊又要一塊。

人對「財、色、名、食、睡」
這五欲也是這樣，
這個也放不下，那個也看不破，
結果就會把自己
弄得好像蠶蟲作繭──
自縛其身，出不來了！

這是誰叫你得不到解脫呢？

繭

Who told them not to seek freedom?

Cocoon

Who told them not to seek freedom?

People crave the five desires.
They believe the five desires are good.
It is just like a child eating candy.
When he finishes one piece,
he wants another.
For people, treating the five desires, wealth, sex,
fame, food and sleep are just the same.
People cannot let go of them
or see through them.
The result is they spin themselves
into a cocoon like a silkworm.
They bind themselves up
and cannot get out.
Who told them not to seek freedom?

我們本有的自性都是清淨的。
但，因為有了貪欲、愛欲、財欲、
才把這清淨的自性都弄得邋遢了。

這一邋遢就變成黑夜茫茫，
沒有智慧，沒有光明了，
常在黑暗的境界裏面見不著光，
生死的疲勞因此而起。

所以——
多欲就是造生死。

Our original nature is pure.

41

Blindness

Our original nature is pure.

Because of greed, desire for love,

desire for wealth, and desire for sex,

we defile our pure nature.

This defilement is as dark as night,

without wisdom and light.

The weariness of birth and death arises

because we cannot find our way

out of this darkness.

So desires create birth and death.

慧

真正的智慧是從什麼地方來的？
是從清淨心生出來的。
又怎麼會現出來清淨心？
就是要「勤修戒定慧，
　　　　　息滅貪瞋痴。」

你若能這樣，
就會現出你清淨的本源妙真如性。

Where does true wisdom come from?

It comes from a pure heart.

How does a pure heart reveal itself?

It comes from practicing precepts,

concentration and wisdom

and cutting off greed,

anger and delusion.

If people can practice like this,

their original, pure, wonderful,

true natures will reveal themselves.

Wisdom

Where does true wisdom come from?

Cause and result are an inevitable part of life.

人在世界上，
什麼奇奇怪怪的事情都有。
為什麼？
因為當初種奇怪的因，
所以現在結奇怪的果。
你若不種這種因，就不會結這種果。
我們若明白因果的道理，
就要「諸惡莫作，眾善奉行」。

世界上的人，
與因果是分不開的。
但是人人都看不見因，只看見果：
當果報到來的時候，
就手忙腳亂不知如何是好。

這都是當初種因時不小心，
等到受奇奇怪怪的果報時，
才覺得莫名其妙。

In the world,

all kinds of strange things happen.

Why?

Because in the past, people planted unusual causes,

now they are reaping strange results.

If people did not plant these causes,

they would not get these results.

If people understand this, they will know,

"Avoid all evil and reverently practice all good."

Cause and result are an inevitable part of life.

But people cannot see causes;

they only see results.

When disappointing results come,

they do not know what to do.

Since they were not careful in planting causes,

when the strange results come, they are baffled.

Causes

人要有慈悲心，
對人對事，要和平相處，以誠相待，
一切替人著想，
不能用毒辣的手段來壓迫人。

學佛法的人，不可撥無因果，
對因果之事，要特別注意！

假如有人對你無理的攻擊，
或用言論來毀謗，
或用行動來迫害，
要處之泰然，不可還擊，
應以慈悲心感化之。

People should use
a compassionate heart to deal
with other people and other matters.
People should interact
with others peacefully and sincerely.
People should think of others
and not oppress them in a vicious manner.
Those studying Buddhism must believe
in cause and result,
and must be careful of cause and result.
If someone attacks you without reason,
or slanders you or oppresses you,
you must deal with it calmly.
Do not return the attacks.
One must use compassion to influence the other
person.

Compassion

仁

我們人時時刻刻都要用慈愛的心，
來愛護一切人。
做事情要衡量衡量，
對自己有利益的事情，不要做那麼多；
對人家有害的事情，更不應該做。
我們若能把
「仁義道德忠孝」這六個字，
推而廣之，擴而充之，
這就是把做人的基礎建立起來。
這樣，你的一生都是健康的，
既身體健康，精神也愉快。
不會憂愁煩惱到髮白、
眼花、耳聾，
可是自己還不覺悟，莫名其妙，
一生很糊塗地就過去了。

Kindness

At all times we should care
for one another with a loving heart.
We should consider things before doing them.
If they benefit us,
we should not spend too much time on them.
If they harm others,
we should not do them at all.
If we can spread the following
six concepts widely—
kindness, righteousness, the Way, virtue,
loyalty and filiality—
then we are building the foundation
for being a human.
In this way our entire lives will be healthy,
and when we are healthy, we are happy.
We will not be melancholy or irritated
and have white hairs,
poor vision or hearing problems.
However, if we don't realize this principle,
then bewildered,
we go through life in a state of confusion.

債

每個人的面目不同，
其因果也不一樣。
每個人在往昔生生世世
所欠下的債也不同。
有的人欠債欠太多了，
到這個世上來，還也還不了，
所謂「債臺高築」
——也就是業障之臺，
一天比一天高，一天比一天深，
債上加債，糾纏不清。
這是什麼緣故呢？
是因為往昔專門放高利貸，
利上加利，
貪得無厭，以為佔了便宜，
結果是自己吃虧
——業障一天比一天重，
結果拔不出腿來。

Debts

People's faces are different,
and their destinies differ.
From countless past lives,
the debts people owe are different.
Some people have huge debts
that they cannot pay off in this lifetime.
They are "up to their ears in debt."
The mountain of debt piles higher
and higher every day.
There is debt upon debt
and they cannot extract themselves from it.
What caused this?
This is because in the past,
they charged high interest.
They charged interest on top of interest.
They were greedy for a good deal.
As a result they are suffering
because their debt is increasing daily
and they can't get out from under it.

人生如演戲，

在這齣戲中，演做皇帝，

享受榮華富貴之樂。

在那齣戲裏，演做乞丐，

受困苦艱難之憂。

做皇帝時，不知乞丐時的苦；

做乞丐時，不知皇帝時的樂。

悲歡離合的境界，

在轉瞬之間，成為一場夢。

自己的業障，增長多少？不知道。

自己的德行，栽培多少？不知道。

不知道，就是無明；

無明，就是生死的根本。

如果沒有無明，便不受六道輪迴之苦。

People's lives are like plays.
Sometimes people play the role of
an emperor and enjoy splendor and riches.
Sometimes people play the role of a beggar
and suffer difficulties and hardships.
When playing the emperor,
one does not know the suffering of the beggar.
When playing the beggar,
one does not know the joys of the emperor.
In the blink of an eye, these states of tragedy
and joy become nothing more than dreams.

Dreams

Do we know how heavy our own karma is?
Do we know how deep our virtue is?
If we do not know, we are ignorant.
Ignorance is the basis of birth and death.
If we can eliminate ignorance,
we will not revolve in the six paths of suffering.

看戲──
不會看的人，
只看戲的節目如何如何，有悲歡離合，
又有一些喜、怒、哀、懼、愛、惡、欲，
就看這些。
明白的人呢？
一看，啊！
原來這些都是如幻如化，人生不過如此！

「一切有為法，如夢幻泡影，
　如露亦如電，應作如是觀。」

Plays

In watching plays,
those who do not understand
just watch the plot.
They see the tragedy
and joy in the story.
They watch for happiness,
anger, sorrow, fear, love, evil, and desire.
People who understand know
what it is all an illusion.
This is all life is
All things are impermanent,
like dreams, illusions, bubbles
or shadows, like dewdrops
or lightning flashes.
Contemplate all dharmas in this way.

師

眾人是我師
我是眾人師
時常師自己
自己是常師

大家都是我的師父，
我也是一般人的師父；
就是大家都是我的教授，
我也是大家的教授，
彼此互相學習，
互相切磋琢磨。
自己又時常要以自己為師，
每一天做個簡短的檢討，
看看今天所行所作是否得當？
是不是都合道理？
是不是有不合道理的地方？
要這麼常常反省。

Teacher

Everyone is my teacher.
I am also everyone's teacher.
That means everyone is my professor,
and I also am everyone's professor.
We should study together
and learn from each other.
We should help each other out
when we encounter difficulties in studying.
We also often have to be our own teacher.
We must examine ourselves every day to see
if our actions are virtuous.
Have our actions been in accord
with principle or not?
We must reflect on our behavior.

Filiality is the soul of heaven and earth.

我們做人的基礎是什麼？
就是仁義道德忠孝。
我們每個人出生以來，
耳濡目染所應該注意的，
就是這個「孝」。
你若能盡孝道，
天主就歡喜你；
你若能盡孝道，菩薩就歡喜你；
你若能盡孝道，佛就歡喜你；
你若能盡孝道，
父母一定不會對你發脾氣的；
你若能盡孝道，
一定不會和兄弟姊妹爭利益。
孝道是天地的靈魂，
是做人的基礎。

What is the foundation for being a human?
It is kindness, righteousness,
the Way, virtue, loyalty and filiality.
When we are born,
we are influenced
by what we see and hear.
We should pay attention to filiality.
If you can practice filiality,
the heavens will be pleased with you.
If you can practice filiality,
the Bodhisattvas
will be pleased with you.
If you can practice filiality,
the Buddhas will be pleased with you.
If you can practice filiality,
your parents
will not become upset with you.
If you can practice filiality,
you will not fight
with your brothers and sisters.
Filiality is the soul of heaven and earth;
it is the basis for being a human.

Filiality

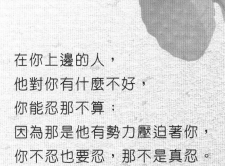

在你上邊的人，
他對你有什麼不好，
你能忍那不算：
因為那是他有勢力壓迫著你，
你不忍也要忍，那不是真忍。

真忍——
就是在你下面的人，
他對你不好，對你污辱，
給你種種的橫逆，
你能忍那才算。

Endurance

Enduring poor treatment from superiors
does not count as true endurance,
because they have the power
to oppress you.
You must endure,
even if you feel you cannot.
That is not true endurance.
Being able to deal
with people under you
when they treat you poorly,
defame you or give you a hard time,
that is true endurance.

喜

做人不要有脾氣，
不要有火氣。
所謂「自古神仙無別法，
　　　廣生歡喜不生愁。」
你若愁一愁，
就跑到地獄裏去遊一遊；
你若笑一笑，就會老返少；
你若哭一哭，
地獄就給你預備個小黑屋；
你樂一樂，
在天堂就有個住處，
它有真正的道理。

Happiness

People
should not have a temper or get angry.
There is an ancient saying,
"The immortals of old had
no other method,
except to always be happy
and never worry."
If you worry too much,
you will go to the hells worrying.
If you laugh a lot, you will not age,
but will stay young.
If you cry a lot, you will find
a little dark room waiting for you in hell.
If you are happy,
you'll find a place in heaven.
There is much truth in these sayings.

我們每一念都要很小心的，
每一念若是善，
則光明越來越多；
但若念惡，則越來越黑暗。
善人有股白光，
惡人有股黑氣，
所以作善作惡，
自然會現出形象出來。
你能瞞得了人，
但瞞不了鬼神、佛菩薩。

所以，修行是
「舉動行為管自己，
行住坐臥不離家。」
要念念清淨，念念光明；
不要念念染污，念念黑暗。

念

Thoughts

We must be careful in every thought.

We must be careful in every thought.
If every thought is benevolent,
then brightness will increase.
If every thought is evil,
then darkness will increase.
Kind people give off a white light.
Evil people emit a black energy.
So whether you do good or evil,
there will be some manifestation.
You might be able to fool people,
but you cannot fool the spirits,
Buddhas, or Bodhisattvas.
Therefore, cultivation means,
"In everything you do,
watch over yourself.
Whether you are moving or still,
awake or asleep,
do not depart from home."
Your thoughts should be pure and bright.
They should not be polluted and dark.

不能來去自如，不能生死自由，
這就是病。
自己做不得主，不能控制長生不老，
這也是病。
若能做得主，可以教身體
眼睛不花、耳朵不聾、
頭髮不白、牙齒不掉嗎？
若沒有這種把握，就是病。

為什麼？因為你心理有病。
有什麼病？有貪的病，
有瞋的病，有癡的病。
貪而無厭，貪求不得，便發脾氣。
那時理智控制不了感情，就糊塗了，
甚至殺人放火，都由此而生，
這不是病是什麼？

病

Illness

If you cannot come and go as you please,
if you are not free to determine
your own birth and death,
then you have an illness.
If you are not your own master,
if you cannot decide your own life span,
you also have an illness.
If you say you are master over your body,
can you tell your eyes not to go bad,
your ears not to go deaf,
your hair not to go white,
your teeth not to fall out?
If you do not have this skill,
then you have an illness.

Why is this? It is because your mind is ill.
How is it ill?
It has the illness of greed, the illness of anger
and the illness of delusion.
When you are insatiably greedy
and unable to obtain what you want,
you lose your temper.
At that point,
reason cannot control your emotions;
you are confused to the point of killing
or committing arson—
all because of greed.
Wouldn't you say that is an illness?

法界佛教總會──簡稱「法總」

· 創辦人──宣化上人。

· 以法界為體,將佛教的真實義理,傳播到世界各地為目的;以翻譯經典、弘揚正法、提倡道德教育、利樂一切有情為己任。

· 以不爭、不貪、不求、不自私、不自利、不妄語為宗旨。

· 有萬佛聖城等近三十座道場,遍佈美、亞洲;其僧眾均須恪遵佛制:日中一食、衣不離體,持戒念佛,習教參禪,和合共住,獻身佛教。

· 有國際譯經學院、法界宗教研究院、僧伽居士訓練班、法界佛教大學、培德中學、育良小學等機構。

· 本會道場、機構,門戶開放,凡各國各教人士,願致力於仁義道德、明心見性者,歡迎前來共同研習!

An Introduction to the Dharma Realm Buddhist Association (DRBA)

- Founder: Venerable Master Hsuan Hua
- Taking the Dharma Realm as its substance, DRBA seeks to disseminate the true principles of Buddhism to all areas of the world. Its missions are to translate the Buddhist scriptures, to propagate the orthodox Dharma, to promote ethics-based education, and to benefit all sentient beings.
- The guiding principles of DRBA are: no contention, no greed,no seeking, no selfishness, no seeking of personal advantage, and no lying.
- In addition to the City of Ten Thousand Buddhas, DRBA has nearly thirty branch monasteries located throughout the United States, Canada and Asia. DRBA'S Sangha members honor the rules and practices

established by the Buddha: eating only one meal a day, always wearing the precept sash, observing the precepts and being mindful of the Buddha, studying the Buddha's teachings, practicing meditation, living together in harmony, and dedicating their lives to Buddhism.

- DRBA'S institutions include the International Institute for the Translation of Buddhist Texts, the Institute for World Religions,the Sangha and Laity Training Programs, Dharma R ealm Buddhist University, Developing Virtue Secondary School, and Instilling Goodness Elementary School.

- The doors of DRBA's monasteries and institutions are open to anyone from any country who wishes to devote themselves to the pursuit of humaneness, justice, and ethics, and the discovery of their true mind.

宣化上人簡傳

來自白雪皚皚的中國東北——長白山區。
十九歲出家修道，發願普渡一切眾生。
一九六二年將正確真實的佛法，
由東方帶到西方——美國。
一九六八年五位美國人在上人座下出家，
是在西方建立三寶的第一人。
「美國法界佛教總會」創辦人，
分支道場遍佈美、加、亞、澳地區。
建立美國第一座佛教大道場——萬佛聖城。
一九九五年圓寂，「我從虛空來，回到虛空去」。
終其一生儘量幫助世界走向安樂光明的途徑，
大慈悲普渡，流血汗，不休息！

A Brief Introduction to
the Venerable Master Xuan Hua

He came from the snow-laden country near the Eternally White Mountains in northeastern China.

At the age of nineteen, he became a Buddhist monk and vowed to save all living beings.

In 1962, he brought the Proper Buddhadharma from East to West (i.e., the U.S.).

In 1968, five Americans took monastic vows under his guidance. Thus, he was the first person to establish the Triple Jewel on American soil.

He founded the Dharma Realm Buddhist Association, with branch monasteries in the United States, Canada, Asia and Australia.

He established the City of Ten Thousand Buddhas, the first large Buddhist monastic community in America

In 1995, before he passed into stillness, he said, "I came from empty space, and to empty space I will return."

Throughout his life, through his own sweat and blood, he helped the world walk towards the path of peace and light, compassionately and tirelessly rescuing living beings.

法界佛教總會・萬佛聖城
Dharma Realm Buddhist Association &
The City of Ten Thousand Buddhas
4951 Bodhi Way, Ukiah, CA 95482 USA
Tel: (707) 462-0939   Fax: (707) 462-0949
http://www.drba.org , www.drbachinese.org

國際譯經學院 **The International Translation Institute**
1777 Murchison Drive, Burlingame, CA 94010-4504 U.S.A.
Tel: (650) 692-5912   Fax: (650) 692-5056

法界宗教研究院（柏克萊寺）
Institute for World Religions(at Berkeley Buddhist Monastery)
2304 McKinley Avenue, Berkeley, CA 94703 U.S.A.
Tel: (510) 848-3440   Fax: (510) 548-4551

金山聖寺 **Gold Mountain Monastery**
800 Sacramento Street, San Francisco, CA 94108 U.S.A.
Tel: (415) 421-6117   Fax: (415) 788-6001

金聖寺 **Gold Sage Monastery**
11455 Clayton Road, San Jose, CA 95127 U.S.A.
Tel: (408) 923-7243   Fax: (408) 923-1064

法界聖城 **City of the Dharma Realm**
1029 West Capitol Avenue, West Sacramento, CA 95691 U.S.A.
Tel/Fax: (916) 374-8268

金輪聖寺 **Gold Wheel Monastery**
235 North Avenue 58, Los Angeles, CA 90042 U.S.A.
Tel/Fax: (323) 258-6668

長堤聖寺 **Long Beach Monastery**
3361 East Ocean Boulevard, Long Beach, CA 90803 U.S.A.
Tel/Fax: (562) 438-8902

華嚴精舍 **Avatamsaka Hermitage**
9601 Seven Locks Road, Bethesda, MD 20817-9997 USA
Tel/Fax: (301) 469-8300

金峰聖寺 **Gold Summit Monastery**
233 First Avenue West, Seattle, WA 98119 U.S.A.
Tel: (206) 284-6690   Fax: (206) 284-6918

金佛聖寺　Gold Buddha Monastery
248 E. 11th Avenue, Vancouver, B.C. V5T 2C3 Canada
Tel: (604) 709-0248　Fax: (604) 684-3754

華嚴聖寺　Avatamsaka Monastery
1009 Fourth Avenue S.W., Calgary, AB T2P 0K8 Canada
Tel/Fax: (403) 234-0644

金岸法界 Gold Coast Dharma Realm
106 Bonogin Road, Mudgeeraba, QLD. 4213 Australia
Tel: (07) 5522-8788; 5520-1188

法界佛教印經會 Dharma Realm Buddhist Books Distribution Society
臺灣省臺北市忠孝東路六段 85 號 11 樓
Tel: (02) 2786-3022, 2786-2474　Fax: (02) 2786-2674

法界聖寺 Dharma Realm Monastery
臺灣省高雄縣六龜鄉興龍村東溪山莊 20 號
Tel: (07) 689-3713　Fax: (07) 689-3870

彌陀聖寺 Amitabha Monastery
臺灣省花蓮縣壽豐鄉池南村四健會 7 號　Tel: (03) 865-1956　Fax: (03) 865-3426

佛教講堂 Buddhist Lecture Hall
香港跑馬地黃泥涌道 31 號 11 樓
31 Wong Nei Chong Road, Top Floor, Happy Valley, Hong Kong, China
Tel: 2572-7644　Fax: 2572-2850

般若觀音聖寺 (紫雲洞)
Prajna Guan Yin Sagely Monastery (Formerly Tze Yun Tung Temple)
Batu 5 1/2, Jalan Sungai Besi, Salak Selatan,
57100 Kuala Lumpur, West Malaysia　Tel: (03)7982-6560 Fax: (03)7980-1272

法界觀音聖寺 (登彼岸)
Dharma Realm Guanyin Sagely Monastery (Formerly Deng Bi An Temple)
161, Jalan Ampang, 50450 Kuala Lumpur, Malaysia
Tel: (03) 2164-8055 Fax: (03) 2163-7118

馬來西亞法界佛教總會檳城分會
Malaysia Dharma Realm Buddhist Association Penang Branch
32-32C, Jalan Tan Sri Teh Ewe Lim,
11600 Jelutong,Penang, Malaysia
Tel: (04)281-7728 Fax: (04)281-7798

出塵 Transcending the World

作　者　宣化上人
攝影者　謝國正、劉法藏、張文星、江明珊、陳德坪等

發行人　法界佛教總會
出　版　法界佛教總會・佛經翻譯委員會・法界佛教大學
　　　　The City of Ten Thousand Buddhas(萬佛聖城)
地　址　4951 Bodhi Way, Ukiah, CA 95482 USA
　　　　Tel: (707) 462-0939　Fax: (707)462-0949
　　　　http://www.drba.org , www.drbachinese.org

　　　　The International Translation Institute
　　　　1777 Murchison Drive Burlingame,
　　　　CA 94010-4504 U.S.A.
　　　　Tel: (650) 692-5912　Fax: (650) 692-5056

倡　印　萬佛聖城　The City of Ten Thousand Buddhas
　　　　4951 Bodhi Way, Ukiah, CA 95482 USA
　　　　Tel: (707) 462-0939　Fax: (707)462-0949

　　　　法界佛教印經會
　　　　Dharma Realm Buddhist Books Distribution Society
　　　　臺灣省臺北市忠孝東路六段 85 號 11 樓
　　　　11th Floor, 85 Chung-hsiao E. Road, Sec. 6,
　　　　Taipei, Taiwan, R.O.C.
　　　　電話: (02) 2786-3022, 2786-2474
　　　　www.drbataipei.org

出版日　2007 年 5 月 2 日・初版三刷
ISBN 978-088139-865-6